T0164996

Other books by Garry Stopa

The Day of Benjamin
More than Enough
Baptized in God

The Gifts
of the
Holy Spirit

Baptism in the Holy Spirit

GARRY STOPA

WestBow
PRESS
A DIVISION OF THOMAS NELSON

All Scripture quotations, unless otherwise indicated, are taken from the New King James Version®. Copyright © 1982 by Thomas Nelson, Inc. Used by permission. All rights reserved.

Scripture quotations marked (KJV) are taken from the Authorized King James Version of the Bible and are public domain.

Scripture quotations marked (NLT) are taken from the Holy Bible, New Living Translation, copyright © 1996, 2004, 2007. Used by permission of Tyndale House Publishers, Inc., Carol Stream, Illinois 60188. All rights reserved.

Scripture quotations marked as such are taken from The Message. Copyright © 1993, 1994, 1995, 1996, 2000, 2001, 2002. Used by permission of NavPress Publishing Group.

Scripture quotations marked (AMP) are taken from the Amplified Bible, Copyright © 1954, 1958, 1962, 1964, 1965, 1987 by The Lockman Foundation. Used by permission.

WestBow Press books may be ordered through booksellers or by contacting:
WestBow Press
A Division of Thomas Nelson
1663 Liberty Drive
Bloomington, IN 47403
www.westbowpress.com
1-(866) 928-1240

ISBN: 978-1-4497-4512-7 (hc)
ISBN: 978-1-4497-4513-4 (sc)
ISBN: 978-1-4497-4514-1 (e)
Library of Congress Control Number: 2012905739

Printed in the United States of America
WestBow Press rev. date: 04/13/2012

Contents

Preface ix

Introduction xi

The Tabernacle 13

Who Is the Holy Spirit? 21

The Holy Spirit and the Tabernacle 29

Three Cups 39

The Three Tribes 55

Access 65

The Body 77

Take Advantage 87

Appendix A 93

    Build Me a Tabernacle 93

    The Grand Tour 93

Appendix B 98

    Let's Talk 98

Appendix C 100

    The Secret Meeting 100

Appendix D 102

    Filling the Cups 102

Appendix E 103

    The Census 103

Appendix F 105

    The Birth of Levi 105

Appendix G 107

    The Perfume Maker 107

For Him

I thank Jesus for every worthwhile achievement in my life. I am grateful for the wonderful wife, children, and grandchildren He has given me. I also thank God for a grace-preaching church that overflows in His love through the people that attend it. My goal is to fulfill His purpose. I have no doubt that this book is part of His plan for me.

Visit my website and connect to my blog to receive weekly inspiration: *www.booksbygarrystopa.com.*

Preface

I believe God wants to take His church up to a new level before His return. God has a custom program for every individual, and He wants to minister to each of us and through each of us.

By learning the characteristics of the Holy Spirit that are addressed in this book, you will have a more personal relationship with your Creator. As God becomes more personal to you, you will become better equipped to fulfill your destiny. As you grow in this knowledge, you will reap a joy that is beyond anything this world has to offer. You will be flooded with peace that passes understanding, and you will learn to recognize God's presence in everything you do.

I pray that as you read this book, you will receive a personal message from God.

Introduction

As with all of my books, I support everything with Scripture references. Some of the teachings are so full of Scripture that I had to put the Scripture references in the back of the book. This makes these lessons easier to digest.

My goal was to make this message as simple as possible to understand. I used a variety of popular Bible translations to express the meaning of each reference in a clear, concise manner. I used several Bible study tools to confirm my interpretations before I included them in this book.

Chapter One

The Tabernacle

And let them make Me a sanctuary, that I may dwell among them.

—Exodus 25:8

1

The Tabernacle

Build Me a Tabernacle[1]

You may be familiar with the famous movie titled The Ten Commandments. Released back in 1956, this movie gave the biblical account of Moses leading Israel out of slavery in Egypt.

Once he was in the wilderness, Moses met with God upon a mountain. Upon that mountain, God gave Moses the Ten Commandments written on stone tablets. The movie did not show it, but Moses also received plans to build a tent-like structure called a tabernacle. This was to be a place for Israel to worship God in their midst.

The Grand Tour[2]

The courtyard appears to be about 75 feet wide and 150 feet deep. There is a seven-and-one-half-foot wall surrounding the courtyard that is prepared from fine woven linen. The entrance is also fine woven linen but it is beautifully embroidered with blue, purple, and scarlet thread. The entrance is on the east side.

As you enter the courtyard from the east, you see beyond the tabernacle that the sun has set. It is twilight, and the evening sacrifice has already begun. The bull on the altar is a sin offering—an

---

[1]   Supporting Scriptures page 93.
[2]   Supporting Scriptures pages 93–97.

innocent animal sacrificed on the altar to pay the price for sin. The smell of roasted meat and baked bread permeates your senses as you walk past the magnificent bronze-plated altar that measures seven-and-a-half feet square and four-and-a-half feet tall.

As you continue along, you pass by a large washbasin that is also plated with bronze. This is where the priests wash their hands and feet so they can enter the tabernacle. The tabernacle from the outside appears to be a tent made from animal skins. Except for the entrance through another set of curtains, exquisitely designed in blue, purple, and scarlet embroidery, there seems to be nothing special about the appearance of this tent-like structure. This seems to be an unusual dwelling place for our creator God.

As you enter the tabernacle, you see something much more extraordinary. Inside this tabernacle, pure gold plating completely covers fifteen-foot-high walls. Gold plating also covers all of the furnishings. To your right is a beautifully decorated table. It measures thirty-six inches by eighteen inches, and it is twenty-seven inches high. On top of the table there are bowls, pans, pitchers, and jars that are all made of pure gold. Also on top of the table are twelve loaves of bread, two bowls filled with frankincense, and a pitcher of wine.

On your left is the lampstand. It consists of one main lamp with three branches off each side, each branch with its own lamp. This lampstand is seventy-five pounds of solid gold. The gold walls and furnishings brilliantly reflect the light provided by the lampstand.

There are more curtains made of finely woven linen thirty feet into the tabernacle. This time the curtains have a pattern somewhat like the wings of a great bird. Just before the curtains stands a small altar for burning incense. The sweet smell of this incense has replaced the aroma of the sacrifice outside. The fragrance fills the tabernacle because there is nowhere for this sweet smell to escape. Also plated in pure gold, the altar for burning incense is thirty-six inches high and eighteen inches square. This is the first section of the tabernacle. The area inside the tabernacle and the courtyard outside is a holy place.

Beyond the curtains is the most holy place. This is where priests meet with God and listen to Him speak. This is where the Ark of the Covenant is located. The ark is like a chest. It contains the tablets with the Ten Commandments written on them. The ark is gold plated, both inside and outside. The ark measures forty-five inches by twenty-seven inches square and twenty-seven inches high. The cover of the ark is completely pure gold. The Bible calls this cover the mercy seat. Rising up from the top of the mercy seat are two birdlike creatures. The wingspan of the birdlike creatures covers the mercy seat. These creatures face each other from opposite sides.

The mercy seat, complete with the two birdlike creatures, is one piece of pure gold. It is illuminated by the glory of God, so there is no need for light in this section of the tabernacle. The glory of God is a powerful light. The wings of the birdlike creatures have to protect the priest who enters into this most holy place. The wings overshadow the intense light that is produced by the presence of God on the mercy seat. Even though the priest has gone through extreme measures to prepare himself, no man is righteous enough to enter the presence of God face to face.

The Cross—the Tabernacle

What does all of this mean? A tabernacle is a tent-like structure used as a dwelling place. This tabernacle was the dwelling place of God in the midst of His chosen people, the Jews. Exodus—chapters 25 through 30—gives you the intricate details about this tabernacle.

God gave Moses the plans for the tabernacle and its furnishings during the forty days he was with God on Mount Sinai. It was where Moses received the Ten Commandments written on stone tablets. God told Moses in Exodus 25:9, "You must build this Tabernacle and its furnishings exactly according to the pattern I will show you" (NLT). The details are important because they give important revelation to the New Testament church.

Everything about the tabernacle points to Jesus. The tabernacle was in the midst of two to three million Jews. An aerial view of the tabernacle with the tribes of Israel around it would reveal the formation of a cross (Num. 2). Every component of the tabernacle has New Testament significance.

First, there was the large altar in the courtyard. This is where an innocent animal received judgment for the sins of the people. The Bible says in 1 Peter 2:24, "[Jesus] Himself bore our sins in His own body on the tree." Jesus became the sacrifice on the cross for our sins instead of an animal on an altar.

Next was the washbasin. The priests had to wash their hands and feet to enter the tabernacle. Ephesians 5:26 says, "That He [Jesus] might sanctify and cleanse her [the church] with the washing of water by the word." Today we wash with the Word of God instead of a washbasin. Inside the tabernacle and to the right was the table with bread and wine, which symbolizes the last supper (Mark 14:22-25). Across from the table and on the left, we have the lampstand that provides light inside the tabernacle. John 1:4 says, "In Him [Jesus] was life, and the life was the light of men." The Holy Spirit in Jesus has become our light. The lampstand signifies the presence of the Holy Spirit.

When one would enter the tabernacle, straight ahead one would see the altar that was used to burn incense. Revelation 5:8 says, "Golden bowls full of incense, which are the prayers of the saints." Our prayers have become a sweet smell to the Lord.

Separated by a curtain, beyond the altar of incense was the most holy place. It is where the glory of God sat upon the mercy seat. The curtain protected sinful man from the glory of God. The Bible tells us in Exodus 33:20, "But He said, 'You cannot see My face; for no man shall see Me, and live.'" This tells us that sin cannot exist in this glory.

The Bible tells us in Matthew 27:51, "Then, behold, the veil of the temple was torn in two from top to bottom; and the earth quaked, and the rocks were split." This happened when Jesus gave up His spirit on the cross. Because Jesus took the judgment for our sins, we can now enter into the most holy place. When Jesus took our sins, He gave us His righteousness. He paid the price for all of our sins, past, present, and future, and washed us clean by shedding His blood.

The Bible tells us in Hebrews 4:16, "Let us therefore come boldly to the throne of grace, that we may obtain mercy and find grace to help in time of need." This says that the mercy seat is the throne of grace. In the righteousness of Jesus, we can talk to God boldly, face to face.

The tabernacle of the Old Testament is the foundation for this book. I have included a simple illustration of the tabernacle on the next page for you to study.

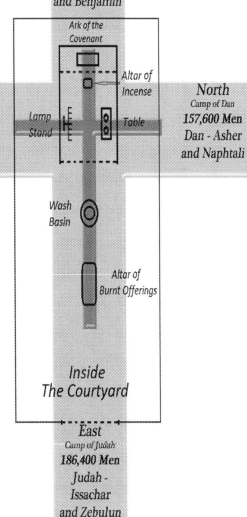

West
Camp of Ephraim
108,100 Men
Ephraim -
Manasseh
and Benjamin

South
Camp of Reuben
141,450 Men
Reuben -
Simeon
and Gad

North
Camp of Dan
157,600 Men
Dan - Asher
and Naphtali

Ark of the
Covenant

Altar of
Incense

Lamp
Stand

Table

Wash
Basin

Altar of
Burnt Offerings

Inside
The Courtyard

East
Camp of Judah
186,400 Men
Judah -
Issachar
and Zebulun

Chapter Two

Who Is the Holy Spirit?

Do not cast me away from Your presence, And do not take Your Holy Spirit from me. Restore to me the joy of Your salvation, And uphold me by Your generous Spirit. Then I will teach transgressors Your ways, And sinners shall be converted to You.

—Psalm 51:11–13

2

Who Is the Holy Spirit?

Let's Talk[3]

It is the eve of the Passover. This is a joyful time for Jewish people. The Passover is a celebration of God's deliverance from slavery in Egypt. This particular Passover is the night that Judas Iscariot will betray Jesus. They will arrest Jesus on this night. Jesus unhindered Judas and sent him along so he might fulfill his evil deeds. Eleven disciples remain at the gathering. Jesus has much to reveal to them, and much of it they will not understand yet.

Jesus tells the disciples, "If you know Me, you know the Father." Philip, one of the disciples, says to Him, "Lord, show us the Father." Jesus answers Philip, "I have been with you so long and yet you do not know Me?" Then Jesus proclaims, "I am in the Father, the Father is in Me and the Father will send you a helper. This helper is the Holy Spirit, and He will come in the name of Jesus." At first this is a little difficult to understand; the Father will send the Holy Spirit in the name of Jesus.

Although much of what Jesus was telling them did not make sense to them right away, eventually they would understand. These are the three personalities of the one and only God. Just as water is frozen, liquid, or gaseous, so God is the Father, Son, and Holy Spirit. God can present Himself as magnificent glory the way He did to Moses on Mount Sinai. God can become a man as Jesus

---

[3]   Supporting Scriptures pages 98–99.

walking the earth. God can even reveal Himself as breath like the Holy Spirit that gave life to Adam.

The Breath of God

In this chapter, we are going to learn about the occupation of the Holy Spirit. When you gain an understanding of *who* the Holy Spirit is, you will better be able to take advantage of everything the Spirit of God has to offer.

As you may know, originally written in Hebrew, the Old Testament Scripture is available in many different languages. Now we can read it in our own language.

The word translated as "Spirit" comes from a Hebrew word pronounced "*roo'-akh*."[4] This word means breath or exhalation. Therefore, Holy Spirit means holy breath or God's breath.

The first mention of God's breath in the Bible is in Genesis 2:7, "And the Lord God formed man *of* the dust of the ground, and breathed into his nostrils the breath of life; and man became a living being." God's breath is the breath of life. All of His attributes are contained in His breath.

The first time we see the Holy Spirit mentioned in The New Testament is Matthew 1:18: "Now the birth of Jesus Christ was as follows: After His mother Mary was betrothed to Joseph, before they came together, she was found with child of the Holy Spirit." Jesus was the child of the Holy Spirit. Since Jesus is the Son of God, this means that the Holy Spirit is God.

Jesus tells us in John 14:26, "But the Helper, the Holy Spirit, whom the Father will send in My name, He will teach you all things, and bring to your remembrance all things that I said to you." According to this passage, God gave us the Holy Spirit to help us.

---

[4]   James Strong, *Strong's Talking Greek and Hebrew Dictionary* (Austin, TX: Wordsearch Corp., 2002), Bible study software, Strong's Number, H7307.

The first time man was given a helper was in Genesis 2:18, where the Bible tells us, "And the Lord God said, '*It is* not good that man should be alone; I will make him a helper comparable to him.'" In the Hebrew language, this helper was a counterpart or opposite.[5] In other words, this helper had everything the man did not have.

The Bible says in John 14:26, "But the Helper, the Holy Spirit . . ." Then it says in Psalm 54:4, "Behold, God *is* my helper." The Helper is the Holy Spirit, and the Helper is God. Now let's look at two more verses. John 4:24 says, "God *is* Spirit." and in 2 Corinthians 3:17 we read, "Now the Lord is the Spirit." God is the Spirit, and the Lord is the Spirit. These verses confirm to us that the *Holy Spirit is God.*

The Bible says in Isaiah 63:11, "Then he remembered the days of old, Moses *and* his people, *saying:* 'Where *is* He who brought them up out of the sea with the *shepherd* of His flock? Where *is* He who put His Holy Spirit within them?'" This verse identifies the Holy Spirit as a shepherd.

The Holy Spirit fulfills the role of a shepherd to meet all of our needs. He protects us and leads us in the way we should go. The Holy Spirit is our complete life source. No matter what our need might be, the Holy Spirit makes us complete, without any lack.

The Holy Spirit is our supply of every good thing. Just as God is the I AM, so is the Holy Spirit (Ex. 3:14). The Holy Spirit can be a mother to the motherless as well as a father to the fatherless.

The Holy Spirit has both male and female attributes. Most passages in the Bible identify the Holy Spirit as a male. However, several passages identify the Holy Spirit as female. We see in Matthew 2:18, "A cry was heard in Ramah—weeping and great

[5] James Strong, *Strong's Talking Greek and Hebrew Dictionary* (Austin, TX: Wordsearch Corp., 2002), Bible study software, Strong's Numbers, H5828, & H5048.

mourning. Rachel weeps for her children, refusing to be comforted, for they are dead" (NLT).

This is a New Testament verse quoting an Old Testament prophecy from the book of Jeremiah (31:15). We know Rachel is the Holy Spirit because Rachel was in Ramah. This word Ramah means, "Elevated grandeur place of excellence."[6] Rachel was in heaven. God would send the Holy Spirit later on after the resurrection of Jesus. The Holy Spirit was crying over the murder of Her children by King Herod. In addition, Genesis 29:6-9 tells us that Rachel was a shepherd to her father's sheep. We already know the Holy Spirit is a shepherd to the Father's sheep.

The Holy Spirit is custom fit for each one of us. The Spirit provides specific help for our own personal needs. The Scripture tells us in Romans 8:26, "Likewise the Spirit also helps in **our** weaknesses" and then goes on to say in 2 Corinthians 12:10, "For when I am weak, then I am strong." This is saying that our personal weaknesses can become our strengths. We just tap into the help available to us from the Holy Spirit.

One of my favorite preachers, Pastor Joseph Prince, had a terrible stuttering problem as a young man. This man is senior pastor at New Creation Church in Singapore. This church now has well over twenty-thousand members, and this man does not stutter any more.

When I received the gift of salvation, I could not read. I would read a few sentences and have to start over because the words just seemed to mix up. It was a real problem when I wanted to read the Bible. I asked God to help me with this problem, and He did more than I expected. Now, not only can I read, but I also write books. In my weakness, He is strong.

The apostle Paul, writing the church at Corinth, told them that there are nine gifts of the Spirit (see 1 Cor. 12:8-10 KJV). The

---

[6]   Roswell D. Hitchcock, *Hitchcock's Bible Names Dictionary* (Austin, TX: Wordsearch Corp, 2002) Bible study software. Name search, *Ramah.*

gifts of the Spirit are wisdom, knowledge, faith, healing, miracles, prophecy, discerning, tongues, and interpretation of tongues.

Paul later told the Galatian church in a letter about nine fruits of the Spirit (see Gal. 5:22-23 KJV). The fruits of the Spirit are love, joy, peace, longsuffering (emotional strength), gentleness, goodness, faithfulness, gentleness, and self-control.

The gifts of the Spirit are essential tools God has provided to benefit the church. The Bible tells us in 1 Corinthians 12:7, "But the manifestation of the Spirit is given to each one for the profit *of all.*"

The Holy Spirit is the complete manifestation of God in Spirit. Jesus Christ made the Holy Spirit available to us by His sacrifice on the cross. God has filled us with His Spirit only because we have received the righteousness of God by this sacrifice.

The Holy Spirit is God. The Holy Spirit reveals Himself through these gifts and fruit. The illustration on the next page is for easy reference.

Gifts	Fruit
Wisdom Knowledge Faith	Love Joy Peace
Healing Miracles Prophecy	Longsuffering Gentleness Goodness
Discernment Tongues Interpretation	Faith Meekness Self-control

Chapter Three

The Holy Spirit and the Tabernacle

And I heard a loud voice from heaven saying, "Behold, the tabernacle of God is with men, and He will dwell with them, and they shall be His people. God Himself will be with them and be their God.

—Revelation 21:3

3

The Holy Spirit and the Tabernacle

The Secret Meeting[7]

As word began to spread about the water being turned into wine and the supernatural signs performed by Jesus, many people believed in Him. There was a Passover celebration taking place, so God was already on their minds. It was a celebration much like our Christmas of today—a time to remember our God-given freedom.

The dark of the night provided an opportunity for Nicodemus to meet with Jesus. It was an opportune time because no other religious leaders would notice. Nicodemus was a Pharisee—a religious leader. Most of the other religious leaders disapproved of Jesus. They insisted that He had to be a fraud. People were turning to Jesus for spiritual guidance instead of them, and they were jealous.

Nicodemus pondered the question, "Who is this man they call Jesus?" He knew Jesus had performed miracles and had been healing all who were sick. He knew that Jesus had even cleansed people from leprosy; even in the Scriptures, this was rare. Surely God had to be with this man.

Nicodemus addressed Jesus as Rabbi, an official title of honor. Jesus responded to Nicodemus, knowing what was on his mind, and declared, "To see the kingdom of God you must be born again." Nicodemus did not understand. Jesus further explained

---

[7]   Supporting Scriptures pages 100–01.

that you have to be born out of water (referring to Noah's waters of judgment) and born of Spirit (the Holy Spirit).

Jesus' crucifixion was payment enough for all humankind. When we receive His payment for our sins, all of the judgment we deserve has been paid for, for all time. Jesus took us out of the waters of judgment. Jesus became our sin offering. Then He washed us of all unrighteousness by the shedding of His blood. The sacrifice of Jesus prepares our bodies to be an acceptable, sanctified environment for the Holy Spirit.

The Tabernacle—a Shadow of the Cross

The Bible tells us in Hebrews 10:1, "For the law, having a shadow of the good things to come and not the very image of the things . . ." The tabernacle of the Old Testament marked the covenant of law. The tabernacle was God's dwelling place and a shadow of things to come. The Bible says in Exodus 25:8, "And let them make Me a sanctuary, that I may dwell among them." The Israelites were freed from slavery in Egypt and were instructed by God to build this tabernacle. We studied the tabernacle in chapter 1.

We read in the New Testament, "For you are the temple of the living God. As God has said: '*I will dwell in them and walk among them. I will be their God, and they shall be My people'*" (2 Cor. 6:16). In the New Testament, *we* are God's dwelling place. We are the temple of the living God, and He dwells in us. The crucifixion of Jesus on the cross made this possible.

We know the tabernacle was a shadow of things to come. A good place to begin our study of the Holy Spirit is to identify His presence at this first dwelling place that was in the *midst of man.*

The Holy Spirit inside the Tabernacle

The Bible makes this reference about Jesus in John 1:4, "In Him was life, and the life was the light of men." The Holy Spirit completely filled Jesus (see Luke 4:1). This tells us that the Holy Spirit is light.

God instructed Moses in Exodus 25:31, "You shall also make a lampstand of pure gold." The lampstand was to provide light. It was to have three branches on each side, and Exodus 25:33 tells us that each of the branches would have three lamp cups shaped like almond blossoms, complete with buds and petals. Take note that each branch has three cups. The number of cups is also an important point. We will discuss this more in the next chapter.

God then told Moses to set the lampstand on the south side of the tabernacle. The light came from the south. I have included the illustration on the next page to help you see this. Pay particular attention to the location of the lampstand.

West

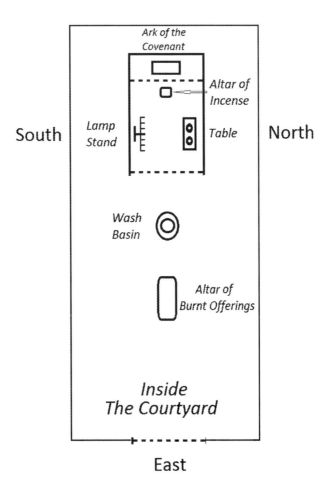

Ark of the Covenant

Altar of Incense

Lamp Stand

Table

South

North

Wash Basin

Altar of Burnt Offerings

Inside The Courtyard

East

The Tabernacle

The lampstand was a light source inside the tabernacle. God told Moses in Exodus 25:37, "You shall make seven lamps for it, and they shall arrange its lamps so that they give light in front of it [toward the table]." When the priest came to the table, he was in the light provided by the lampstand.

The table inside the tabernacle had bread on it. This signified communion or fellowship with God. When we spend time with God's Word or listening to preaching, the Holy Spirit brings light to the Word of God.

The Holy Spirit outside of the Tabernacle

The tabernacle also revealed the presence of the Holy Spirit on the outside. You have noticed that the lampstand was along the south wall of the tabernacle.

The tribes of Israel were camped outside of the tabernacle. The size of each camp exposes the formation of a cross (see Num. 2). Camped outside and to the south were the tribes of Reuben, Simeon, and Gad (Num. 2:10-14). The Holy Spirit is "The Queen of the South" in Matthew 12:42. This Scripture in Matthew is referring to the Holy Spirit. She is the Queen of these tribes.

The Holy Spirit is on the south side of the tabernacle. On the inside, the lampstand reveals the Holy Spirit, but the names of these three tribes and their leaders reveal Him on the outside.

The illustration on the next page reveals the names of each tribe. Another significant point here is that there are three tribes on the south. We will be discussing this detail later in this book.

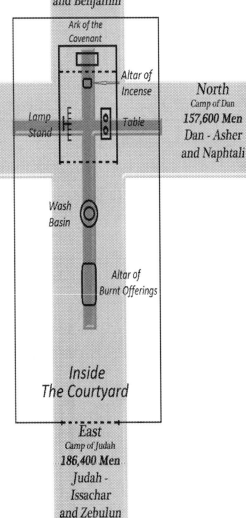

West
Camp of Ephraim
108,100 Men
Ephraim -
Manasseh
and Benjamin

South
Camp of Reuben
141,450 Men
Reuben -
Simeon
and Gad

North
Camp of Dan
157,600 Men
Dan - Asher
and Naphtali

Ark of the
Covenant

Altar of
Incense

Lamp
Stand

Table

Wash
Basin

Altar of
Burnt Offerings

*Inside
The Courtyard*

East
Camp of Judah
186,400 Men
Judah -
Issachar
and Zebulun

The name of each tribe and its leader reveals something very interesting. The first tribe on the south side is Reuben. The Bible says in Numbers 2:10, "On the south side shall be the standard of the forces with Reuben according to their armies, and the leader of the children of Reuben shall be Elizur the son of Shedeur."

The name Reuben means, "See ye a Son," the name Elizur means "God of the Rock," and Shedeur means "Spreader of Light."[8]

When we translate these Hebrew names to English, the sentence says, "See the Son, the God of the Rock, the Son of the Spreader of Light." In other words, the Holy Spirit on the outside of the tabernacle reveals Jesus, the Son of God.

The Bible tells us in Numbers 2:12, "Those who camp next to him [Reuben] *shall be* the tribe of Simeon, and the leader of the children of Simeon *shall be* Schelumiel the son of Zurishaddai." The name Simeon means "Hearing," Schelumiel means "Peace of God," and Zurishaddai means "Rock of Almighty[9]." This repeats a similar message to the last one, except now it reveals Jesus as the peace of God. The Bible tells us in John 3:17, "For God did not send His Son into the world to condemn the world, but that the world through Him might be saved." Jesus did not come to condemn the world, as many people wrongfully believe. Jesus came to provide us the *peace of God* that passes all understanding (Phil. 4:7).

The Scripture goes on to tell us, "Then *comes* the tribe of Gad, and the leader of the children of Gad *shall be* Eliasaph the son of Reuel" (Num. 2:14). Gad means, "Troops," Eliasaph

---

[8] James Strong, *Strong's Talking Greek and Hebrew Dictionary* (Austin, TX: Wordsearch Corp., 2002), Bible study software, Strong's numbers, H7205, H468, & H7707

[9] Strong's numbers, H8095, H8017, & H6701.

means, "Increase," and Reuel means "Knowledge of God."[10] This message says, "The troops are led by an increase in the knowledge of God." On the outside, the Holy Spirit is to teach the troops about Jesus.

In simple terms, inside of the tabernacle we received the Holy Spirit as light. Outside of the tabernacle, we release the Holy Spirit as light. The New Testament reveals how the Holy Spirit inside of us is for ourselves; the Holy Spirit outside of us is for others. We will look at this in the next few chapters.

---

[10] James Strong, *Strong's Talking Greek and Hebrew Dictionary* (Austin, TX: Wordsearch Corp., 2002), Bible study software, Strong's numbers, H1410, H460, & H7467

Chapter Four

Three Cups

I am the vine, you are the branches. He who abides
in Me, and I in him, bears much fruit; for without
Me you can do nothing.

—John 15:5

Three Cups

Filling the Cups[11]

It is daybreak; outside of the tabernacle, the priests are preparing the animal sacrifice and grain offering on the altar. The linen curtains at the entrance to the tabernacle are drawn wide open, bringing in the light from the risen sun. Inside the tabernacle, the priests are burning incense, as they always do while they tend to the lampstand. The lampstand needs fresh oil because it has been burning all night. Each branch of the lamp has three bowls. The priest pours freshly pressed olive oil into each bowl. The oil is the fuel for the lamps. The priest will light these lamps again at twilight.

Born of the Spirit

Jesus said in John 3:5, "Most assuredly, I say to you, unless one is born of water and the Spirit, he cannot enter the kingdom of God." This is born again. To be born of the Spirit is the gift of salvation. For us to be an acceptable environment for the Spirit to dwell in, our bodies had to be prepared in the same way a priest had to be prepared. The priest had to go through a process to clean himself of sin and put himself in right standing with God. This enabled him to enter the presence of the Holy Spirit. When Jesus said we had to be born of water, this meant we needed to saved

---

[11]   Supporting Scriptures page 102.

from judgment. Judgment would have destroyed us in the same way the waters destroyed the people on the earth during the great flood of Noah's time. The sacrifices performed by the priests saved them from judgment in the same way.

Preparation

The priest of the Old Testament was required to perform three sacrifices to be sanctified or sinless enough to enter into the most holy place. The Bible says in Exodus 29:1, "And this is what you shall do to them to hallow them for ministering to Me as priests: Take one young bull and two rams without blemish."

The first offering, the bull, was a sin offering. The priest would lay his hands on this offering, transferring his sin onto the innocent animal. The animal then took his place on the altar to receive judgment (see Ex. 29:10-14). The Bible says in 1 Peter 2:24, "[Jesus] bore our sins in His own body on the tree." This tells us that Jesus was our sin offering.

The second offering—the first ram—was a burnt offering. The priest took on the innocence of the animal when he laid hands on it. This offering was a sweet smell to the Lord on the altar (see Ex. 29:15-18). The Bible tells us in Ephesians 5:2, "As Christ also has loved us and given Himself for us, an offering and a sacrifice to God for a sweet-smelling aroma." This tells us that Jesus was also our burnt offering.

The third offering—the second ram—was a consecration offering. The Bible says in Leviticus 8:22, "And he brought the second ram, the ram of consecration. Then Aaron and his sons laid their hands on the head of the ram." The Hebrew word translated as consecration means fulfillment.[12] It was an offering announcing,

---

[12] James Strong, *Strong's Talking Greek and Hebrew Dictionary* (Austin, TX: Wordsearch Corp., 2002), Bible study software, Strong's number, H4394.

"It is finished." The Bible says in John 19:30, "So when Jesus had received the sour wine, He said, 'It is finished!' And bowing His head, He gave up His spirit." This would indicate that the complete fulfillment had been satisfied.

The Bible says in Hebrews 10:14, "For by one offering He has perfected forever those who are being sanctified." According to Revelation 1:6, Jesus has made *us* to be priests (and kings). This means He had to provide all three offerings at the same sacrifice.

The Scripture tells us Jesus hung on the cross for six hours. The Bible says in Mark 15:25, "Now it was the third hour, and they crucified Him." Mark goes on to say, "Now when the sixth hour had come, there was darkness over the whole land until the ninth hour" (Mark 16:33). This means that the first three hours were daylight, and the last three hours were dark. According to Exodus 29, offerings were to take place at morning and evening. The daylight and darkness periods on the cross indicate a morning and an evening sacrifice, the first two offerings.

The Bible tells us that the Lord visits, "the iniquity of the fathers on the children to the third and fourth generation" (Num. 14:18). This means the bondage of sins committed by the fathers infects several generations. The Bible reiterates this in Ezekiel 18:2, "The fathers have eaten sour grapes, And the children's teeth are set on edge?" The children had to drink sour wine for sins of their father. When Jesus tasted the sour wine, He made the final payment.

The first offering paid for our sin. The second offering gave us His righteousness. The third sacrifice was for the sins of our fathers. The Bible says in Exodus 29:26, "Then you shall take the breast of the ram of Aaron's consecration and wave it as a wave offering before the Lord; and it shall be your portion." After they sacrificed this final offering, they were to lift this offering up and wave it. In John 20:17, the Bible says, "Jesus said to her [Mary], 'Do not cling to Me, for I have not yet ascended to My Father; but go to My brethren and say to them, "I am ascending to My Father and your Father, and *to* My God and your God."'" Jesus had to be raised from the dead and lifted up into heaven. In this way, Jesus was waved to complete this final offering. This is why it is so important for us to believe that God raised Jesus from the dead (Rom. 10:9).

This sacrifice of Jesus on the cross cleansed us and prepared us to be a dwelling place for God. The Bible tells us in 1 Corinthians 3:16, "Do you not know that you are the temple of God and *that* the Spirit of God dwells in you?" This means we are born of the Spirit. The birth of the Holy Spirit has taken place inside of us. This was only possible because of the sacrifice of perfect righteousness. There is nothing else as perfect as God Himself.

To receive this gift, the Bible says in Romans 10:9, "That if you confess with your mouth the Lord Jesus and believe in your heart that God has raised Him from the dead, you will be saved." If you believe in the cross, just confess Jesus as Lord to receive complete salvation. He immediately enters us, and we become a dwelling place for the Holy Spirit. We have met all qualifications.

The Spirit Inside

When he was first presented in the tabernacle of Israel, the Holy Spirit revealed Himself as light. This was the light provided by the lampstand. This lampstand had three branches that extended out of each of the two sides. The Bible tells us in Exodus 25:33 that each of these branches had three cups filled with oil. Jesus said He is the vine and we are the branches. We each receive three cups of oil the moment we are born of the Spirit.

We know that Jesus was born of the Spirit because Matthew 1:18 says that Mary was found "with child of the Holy Spirit."

The Bible gives us a demonstration of the Holy Spirit working in Jesus when He was only twelve years old. In Luke 2:46-47 we read, "They found Him in the temple, sitting in the midst of the teachers, both listening to them and asking them questions. And all who heard Him were astonished at His understanding and answers." The Bible goes on to say in verse 52, "And Jesus increased in wisdom and stature, and in favor with God and men." We can expect these results from being born of the Spirit.

The Bible says in Proverbs 8:14, "Counsel *is* mine, and sound wisdom . . ." Jesus displayed God's counsel and sound wisdom when his parents found Him in the temple. This is a demonstration of the first cup—wisdom.

A Cup of Wisdom

The Bible says in Proverbs 8:12, "I, wisdom, dwell with prudence and find out knowledge of witty inventions" (KJV). I really like this verse because I have invented something.

When the idea for the invention first came to me, I gave credit to God, but I did not appreciate just how much was Him. The idea seemed so simple to me.

At the time, I did not feel I had the resources to market the product and get patents. I decided to collaborate with my employer (at the time).

The idea was a good one, but the product needed more development. My partner was a brilliant man, and he had someone on staff who should have been qualified to engineer a unit that could be mass produced and practical for marketing. I was happy to let my partner invest his money into the project; this was included in the partnership agreement that we had.

After about six months and thousands of dollars, they still did not have a practical device to market. I could not believe how difficult it was for them. My partner was doing the coaching, and the engineers (now there were two) were attempting to fulfill his requests.

Developing the device on my own seemed to make more sense. After two days, I had a finished product. My (God's) design is being manufactured and distributed worldwide today.

As I look back on all of this, I realize the Holy Spirit can be so very subtle. The original idea was perhaps simple, but the process of bringing it to market could not have happened without help from the Holy Spirit.

My partner and his development team, who were nonbelievers, just did not have God's wisdom inside them for this project. I know that this invention is 100 percent from the Holy Spirit. I know this because the other people involved in the project should have been qualified to bring this witty invention to market. They could not do it because the Holy Spirit did not give them the ability. The whole experience made me realize how the Holy Spirit can make things seem so simple. He will work through you even if you are not aware that he is doing it.

If you have the Holy Spirit in you, then you have wisdom dwelling in you too. If you have a good idea, then you should do something with it. If the Holy Spirit is involved, then the idea itself will seem simple.

God wants to bless you, and He will give you the resources as you need them, step by step. Never look at the size of the project as a whole; just look at the next step. He will always be there to help when you have to do things that need His help.

The Spirit gives us light to God's Word. Notice that when Jesus was twelve years old, His wisdom increased *as* they were discussing the Word of God.

In the tabernacle, the Holy Spirit provided light in front of the table. This table represents communion or fellowship with God. When we study God's Word, we are fellowshipping with God. Study and speak about God's Word regularly if you want to increase in wisdom.

During church, I have often received a message that was different from what the pastor was preaching. The pastor may quote a Bible passage that triggers something inside of me. This is a personal message revealed to me by the Holy Spirit. Fellowshipping with God by hearing His Word preached activates the Holy Spirit within us.

You may have had the experience of receiving a revelation yourself. If you try to share it, nobody else will get excited about it like you do. This is the result of the Holy Spirit delivering a personal message to you.

Wisdom also allows God to work through us. The Bible teaches us in 1 John 4:19, "We love each other because he loved us first" (NLT). Love is the fruit of wisdom. Wisdom provides a source of God's love on the inside of us.

The Scripture tells us in Romans 5:5, "The love of God has been poured out in our hearts by the Holy Spirit who was given to us." Wisdom and love are harmonious. God poured love-producing wisdom into our cup. Love is very powerful, and a wise man will use it.

Love is our weapon against fear. First John 4:18 tells us, "There is no fear in love; but perfect love casts out fear." Love is a fruit that will also fall onto those in our presence.

A Cup of Knowledge

Jesus declares to us in John 14:26, "The Helper, the Holy Spirit, whom the Father will send in My name, He will teach you all things, and bring to your remembrance all things that I said to you." To teach is to cause someone to know something.

Notice that the Holy Spirit is our Helper. He does not force Himself into our lives. He is available to us as our Helper. Our goal is to know the Holy Spirit personally so we can tap into everything He has to offer. If we know how to identify Him, we can rely on Him for our specific needs.

This passage in John 14 also tells us that the Holy Spirit teaches us *all things*. We know the Holy Spirit is God, and He knows all things. The Bible also says we have the mind of Christ (1 Cor. 2:16). If you have received the gift of salvation, then you literally have the mind of God dwelling inside of you. This is the cup of knowledge provided by the Holy Spirit.

For quite some time, I have asked God to show me things the way He sees them. I go to church and see my brothers and sisters in Jesus. People are so beautiful when you identify the presence of God in them. It is truly an answer to prayer.

One day I was pondering in my thoughts just what a wonderful gift it is to see God in so many people. As I was thinking about this, I heard in my mind, *To see what I see is wonderful, but I also want you to think like me.*

The Bible makes it very clear that as a child of God, all of God is dwelling inside of you, so regularly ask God to blend His thoughts into your thoughts.

During the publication of an earlier book I wrote titled *More Than Enough*, I had just received a proof copy to read before the final print. I was listening to some preaching and heard something very interesting I wanted to add to my book. I had already received the proof, so it was really too late to make that big of a change.

The next day I had my chance to read the proof, and much to my surprise, the references I wanted to add were already in the book. What a demonstration of God flowing through me when I write books.

The Bible tells us in Philippians 2:13, "For it is God who works in you both to will and to do for *His* good pleasure." The word *in* comes from a Greek word that can also mean *through*[13]. The Holy Spirit is God working through you.

To activate the Holy Spirit, you just need to ask him. Remember that the Holy Spirit is our helper. As a helper, He is there to help, but typically He waits for you to ask for His help.

First John 5:6 says, "The Spirit is truth." Scripture tells us in John 16:13 that the Spirit of truth will guide you, and He will tell you of things to come. The Holy Spirit who knows all things, past, present, and future is inside you.

Every day I like to ask God to prepare me for my day ahead and for encounters with other people. I pray that all of the people

---

[13] James Strong, *Strong's Talking Greek and Hebrew Dictionary* (Austin, TX: Wordsearch Corp., 2002), Bible study software, Strong's number, G1722.

I encounter are prepared as well. I also ask for His wisdom to be rooted into every decision I make. Then I rely on Him to guide me down the right paths.

The Bible says in Ecclesiastes 9:11, "The race *is* not to the swift, Nor the battle to the strong, Nor bread to the wise, Nor riches to men of understanding, Nor favor to men of skill; But time and chance happen to them all."

Rather than relying on our own abilities, we can take advantage of the Holy Spirit putting us in the right place at the right time. I ask for this regularly too.

You must remember that He is a real person. You should talk to Him the same way you talk to any person. The more you talk to Him, the more you will know Him.

One day I was really feeling pressure from all the circumstances in life. I thought to myself, *If I am a child of God, why should these circumstances be weighing me down?* I inquired of the Holy Spirit, and in my thoughts I heard, *Pray for joy in the storms.*

Ecclesiastes 2:26 tells us, "For *God* gives wisdom and knowledge and joy to a man who *is* good in His sight." Every child of God is good in His sight.

Joy is a very powerful force. The Bible says in Colossians 1:11, "Strengthened with all might, according to His glorious power, for all patience and longsuffering with joy."

You can more clearly understand this quote from Colossians if you move the word joy to follow the word power. It then reads, "Strengthened with all might, according to His glorious power *of joy* for all patience and longsuffering." Therefore, another way to read this verse is, *strengthened with joy.*

To support this, we also see in Nehemiah 8:10, "Do not sorrow, for the joy of the Lord is your strength."

The cup of knowledge releases this power of joy into your storms. Acts 13:52 says, "And the disciples were filled with joy and with the Holy Spirit."

When we experience joy, it will overflow into those around us. Knowledge produces the fruit of joy.

A Cup of Faith

Another cup of the Holy Spirit inside of us is faith. The apostle Paul said in Romans 12:3, "God has dealt to each one a measure of faith." Then again he says in Ephesians 2:8, "For by grace you have been saved through faith, and that not of yourselves; *it is* the gift of God." Then the apostle Peter wrote, "This faith was given to you" (2 Peter1:1 NLT). Faith is a gift from God.

Hebrews 11 lists off the most prominent people of faith from Old Testament times. These people are famous for standing in faith through some very challenging circumstances. The last two verses of this chapter reveal something even better for the body of Christ. Hebrews 11:39-40 says, "All these people earned a good reputation because of their faith, yet none of them received all that God had promised. For God had something better in mind for us, so that they would not reach perfection without us" (NLT). In other words, we have received a *better* faith so we can reach perfection. We have received the same faith as Jesus.

When I believe for something that is bigger than I can grasp, I simply stand on the fact that the faith inside of me is more than enough. If my faith is weak, I remind myself that God's faith is not weak, and I let Him do His thing. I simply have to know what He said. The Bible gives us an excellent example of this. The Scripture tells us in Luke 5:4-6, "When He had stopped speaking, He said to Simon, 'Launch out into the deep and let down your nets for a catch.' But Simon answered and said to Him, 'Master, we have toiled all night and caught nothing; nevertheless at Your word I will let down the net.' And when they had done this, they caught a great number of fish, and their net was breaking." Notice that Simon (Peter) did not have any faith. He only knew what Jesus said. We have Jesus inside of us; therefore, we have His faith inside of us too.

I do not have to have the faith of Abraham. I am not afraid to say that my own faith is weak. The Holy Spirit's faith is more than enough. Spend time in the Word to know what Jesus has to say about all of your circumstances. We do not even have to have faith in what the Word says; just like Simon Peter, we just have to believe that God said it. This is what grace is all about. If we had enough faith on our own, we would not need His faith. This is why He gave us the gift of faith.

As King David declared, "*God* has broken through my enemies *by my hand* like a flood." (1 Chron. 14:11). The task is simple for the Holy Spirit. When you realize that all you have to do is lift up your hand and declare the Word of God into your situation, you will see Him break through your enemies like a flood. You will see Him move the mountains and calm the storms. Understanding this will bring you into the peace of God.

The Bible says in Romans 15:13, "May the God of hope fill you with all joy and peace." Peace will come when you grasp that your faith is a gift. It is the same faith Jesus had.

Jesus told us in John 14:27, "Peace I leave with you, My peace I give to you; not as the world gives do I give to you. Let not your heart be troubled, neither let it be afraid." Essentially Jesus said His peace is not the same as worldly peace. It is the same way with faith because Jesus's faith is not the same as human faith.

The apostle Paul wrote in Philippians 4:7, "And the peace of God, which surpasses all understanding, will guard your hearts and minds through Christ Jesus." Notice again that the work of the Spirit is inside you guarding your heart and mind.

Just like joy, peace is also fruit of the Spirit. Jesus said in Matthew 10:13, "If the household is worthy, let your peace come upon it. But if it is not worthy, let your peace return to you." Jesus said this again in Luke 10:6, "And if a son of peace is there, your peace will rest on it; if not, it will return to you." Therefore, peace also falls on people who come into your presence, just like the rest of the fruit.

I continually ask the Holy Spirit to saturate me with these wonderful attributes. I want to be like a sponge that takes on more moisture than it can handle. When people come into my presence, I want them to sense His presence and bring Him glory.

In Isaiah 62:7 we see, "Give the Lord no rest until he completes his work" (NLT). Ask the Holy Spirit for everything He has to give. You will grow to be a product of His work and become attractive to both God and man. The Holy Spirit does all of the work. Anything worthwhile we achieve is His doing, and with His help, we can accomplish anything.

To summarize this chapter, we looked at what the Holy Spirit does for us as soon as we are born again. He works inside us as our helper. He gives us wisdom, revelation knowledge, and faith that others can see in us. These gifts overfill us with love, joy, and peace that can fall onto others like fruit.

The three cups on each branch of the lampstand represent the three gifts of the Holy Spirit inside every believer who receives the gift of salvation.

As we learn what was given to us, we can take advantage of it. He can put us in the right place at the right time and make us strong in all of our weaknesses. He is there to help us any time we ask.

If someone put five million dollars into a special bank account for you and did not tell you, the money would not do you any good. Pray continually for wisdom, knowledge, and faith. These gifts are in your bank account, ready for you to withdraw. We need to take advantage of these three gifts and the fruit each one produces.

Gifts	Fruit
Wisdom Knowledge Faith	Love Joy Peace

Chapter Five

The Three Tribes

But you shall receive power when the Holy Spirit has come upon you; and you shall be witnesses to Me in Jerusalem, and in all Judea and Samaria, and to the end of the earth.

—Acts 1:8

5

The Holy Spirit Outside

The Census[14]

Moses had completed the Tabernacle according to all the Lord commanded. Moses waited for the next set of directives from God. The God of the all creation instructed Moses to take a census of all the men ages twenty years and older who were fit to do battle, so Moses counted the men according to their tribe. All of the men of at least twenty years of age were included who were suited for battle.

Next Moses had to arrange the tribes surrounding the tabernacle. Moses was standing at the gates to the court before the leaders of each tribe. He pointed east and declared, "First Judah, then Issachar, and next to Issachar, Zebulun." Moses then pointed to his right and announced, "Reuben to the south, next to Reuben shall be Simeon and next to Simeon shall be the tribe of Gad."

There were thirteen tribes in total. One tribe, the tribe of Levi, was to surround the tabernacle. They were in charge of the tabernacle and all of its furnishings.

Why were all of these details so important? Perhaps it held no significance at the time, but it was prophetic of our covenant with Jesus. Every specific detail revealed a revelation of the crucifixion that took place fourteen hundred years later. We can see now that the arrangement of the tribes during the census formed the pattern of a cross.

---

[14]   Supporting Scriptures pages 103–04.

We have already discussed how the Holy Spirit works inside us as our helper. In this chapter, we will study what the Holy Spirit can do on the outside of us.

Every detail of the tabernacle was a revelation. We have discovered that Scripture discloses certain messages in the names of each tribe. The tribes to the south signified the Holy Spirit because the Holy Spirit was inside the tabernacle along the south wall. The light of the lampstand symbolized the Holy Spirit inside; outside, She is the Queen of the south (Matt. 12:42, Luke 11:31).

The Bible shows us that on the south of the temple was the camp of "Reuben led by Elizur the son of Shedeur." If we look at the *Strong's Greek and Hebrew Dictionary* and translate these names to English, we will discover a hidden message in this sentence. In simple English, the sentence reads, "See the Son, the God of the Rock, and the Son of the Spreader of Light."[15] We will see how this is the function of the Holy Spirit outside of the temple.

The Bible tells us in Luke 3:22, "And the Holy Spirit descended in bodily form like a dove upon Him, and a voice came from heaven which said, 'You are My beloved Son; in You I am well pleased.'" This is talking about Jesus. This happened when John baptized Him in the Jordan River.

We know that Jesus was born of the Spirit, and now we see where the Spirit came upon Him. This took place just before He began His ministry.

The Bible goes on to say in Luke 4:1, "Then Jesus, being filled with the Holy Spirit, returned from the Jordan and was led by the Spirit into the wilderness." The word translated as "filled" comes from a Greek word pronounced "play'-race." According to *Strong's*

---

15   James Strong, *Strong's Talking Greek and Hebrew Dictionary* (Austin, TX: Wordsearch Corp., 2002), Bible study software, Strong's numbers, H7205, H468, & H7707.

Dictionary, this word means, "Well supplied, filled and covered over."[16]

So Jesus was born of the Holy Spirit (Matt. 1:18), and now the Spirit was upon Him. This made Him well supplied, filled, and covered over. He went into the wilderness and fasted for forty days, led by the Holy Spirit inside of Him.

When Jesus returned from the wilderness, He began to preach. He began His ministry of teaching in the Jewish places of worship (synagogues).

He launched His own ministry, declaring these words in Luke 4:18, "The Spirit of the Lord is upon Me, because He has anointed Me to preach the gospel to the poor; He has sent Me to heal the brokenhearted, to proclaim liberty to the captives and recovery of sight to the blind, to set at liberty those who are oppressed." He was quoting from Isaiah 61:1-2.

The word anointed comes from a Greek word pronounced "khree'-o." According to *Strong's Dictionary*, this word means, "to smear or rub with oil (by implication)."[17] The priest would be anointed with oil before he could enter the tabernacle, God instructed Moses to, "take the anointing oil, pour *it* on his [the priest's] head, and anoint him" (Ex. 29:7) God would provide healing, miracles, and prophecy through a priest.

Jesus already had the Spirit inside of Him from birth. This gave Him great wisdom and favor. Now He had the Spirit on the outside of Him to deliver healing, miracles, and prophecy.

The Scripture tells us that Jesus had the Spirit without measure (John 3:34). We are members of one body—the body of Christ (1 Cor. 12:27). The Spirit is in the body of Christ without measure in the same way. However, as individuals, we also receive a measure of the Spirit.

---

[16] James Strong, *Strong's Talking Greek and Hebrew Dictionary* (Austin, TX: Wordsearch Corp., 2002), Bible study software, Strong's number, G4134.

[17] Strong's number, G5548.

The gifts that are available to us because the Holy Spirit is upon us are for the benefit of many. For this reason, we see the Holy Spirit outside of the tabernacle as tribes. Every child of God who has the Spirit upon him or her becomes a contact point for God to bless many. God uses them for the saved as well as to attract people into the kingdom of God. We could consider these gifts to be ministry gifts.

To learn what these manifestations of the Spirit are, we look to the ministry of Jesus. When the Holy Spirit comes upon us, we have the same Spirit Jesus had upon Him.

The First Tribe—Healing

The first ministry gift we will look at is the gift of healing. The first four books of the New Testament are the gospels. The gospels teach us about the ministry of Jesus before His resurrection from the grave. Since it was before He laid down His life, it was still a time under the law covenant. Jesus was the only person born of the Holy Spirit at this point in time. According to the book of Romans, Jesus was the firstborn of many (Romans 8:29).

The gospels are the place to study the ministry of Jesus. We will begin by looking at Matthew 8. This chapter begins by telling about a man healed of leprosy. The man instantly received healing when Jesus touched him.

The second person healed in this chapter was the servant of a Roman captain. This Roman captain was not Jewish. At that time, Jews were the only ones who were considered to be God's children. This healing took place without Jesus even meeting the sick person. Jesus only had to declare it, and the man received healing.

The next person who was healed was the mother-in-law of the apostle Peter. She was sick in bed with a fever. Jesus laid His hands on her, and the fever left. The Bible does not say she was fully recovered; it just says the fever left and she was well enough to serve. There are situations where a complete healing does not appear to happen immediately.

The Bible tells us in verse 16, "And He cast out the spirits with a word, and healed all who were sick." I would consider any kind of demon possession to be an illness because demons can sometimes be the cause of the illness. Healing is available for physical and emotional illnesses no matter what their cause.

To summarize Matthew 8, we can see that healings may or may not be instant, the person may or may not be present, and the person may or may not be a child of God. This gift of the Spirit can heal any type of sickness, whether emotional or physical, and it does not matter what caused the ailment.

Jesus healed people from leprosy, blindness, deafness, paralysis, crippling diseases, demon possession, and much more. Jesus also restored limbs (Matt. 15:30-31) and even raised three people from the dead (Matt. 9:25, Luke 7:15, John 11:44).

When people receive a supernatural healing from God, they always come out stronger. They come out better equipped to handle the next trial they may have to endure. Healing produces the fruit of longsuffering. Longsuffering does not sound like something you would want, but it actually is. This word means emotional strength to face the challenges we face in life[18].

The Second Tribe—Miracles

The next ministry gift we will study is the ministry of miracles. A miracle was the first supernatural display of the Holy Spirit upon Jesus. Jesus turned water into wine. During a wedding celebration, the wine ran out. It must have been a huge wedding, because Jesus turned about 150 gallons of water into wine. We read about this in John 2:1-10. The Bible tells us in John 2:11 "This miraculous sign

---

[18] James Strong, *Strong's Talking Greek and Hebrew Dictionary* (Austin, TX: Wordsearch Corp., 2002), Bible study software, Strong's number, G3115.

at Cana in Galilee was the first time Jesus revealed his glory. And his disciples believed in him" (NLT).

You can see how this influenced the disciples. Because the Holy Spirit fell upon Him, Jesus had the ability to perform miracles. This was the Spirit outside for the purpose of blessing people and drawing them to God.

The ministry of miracles has produced some of the most famous stories in the Bible. For example, once Jesus fed five thousand people with five loaves and two fish. This story is in all four gospels. We find the first account of this story in Matthew 14:15-21.

Another miracle performed by Jesus was when he filled Peter's nets with fish. He performed this miracle twice (Luke 5:6, John 21:6). Jesus walked on water. Matthew, Mark, and John all give accounts of this. Matthew tells us that Peter also walked on the water (Matt. 14:29). In the account given by John (John 6:21), the boat immediately arrived at the other side of the sea.

This story took place during a sudden storm. The Bible says, "Then he climbed into the boat, and the wind stopped. They were totally amazed" (Mark 6:51, NLT).

Every miracle performed by Jesus displays the fruit of gentleness (kindness). Every miracle was a help. Each time it was an act of kindness. The Holy Spirit will never perform a miracle for any other reason.

The Third Tribe—Prophecy

The third ministry gift we will look at is prophecy. The prophecies of our current times have several advantages over the prophecies before the cross. For one thing, we have the Bible available for us to confirm if they are truly from God. We are also in a period of grace, so a prophecy will never condemn. A prophecy will always have a good conclusion.

There is a concentration of prophecies made by Jesus in Matthew 24. Starting in verse 2, Jesus tells His disciples how the old church will be destroyed. This was symbolic of a new church of grace rather than one of law. Next, beginning at verse 4, He warns them of deceivers who will come in the name of Jesus. It seems that a prophecy can reveal future events to redirect us away from danger.

The next prophecy reveals the hardship the disciples will face as they establish the New-Testament church. Then the Bible tells us in Matthew 24:13, "But he who endures to the end shall be saved." This was meant to give the disciples encouragement through the trials they were about to face.

The prophecies to follow in this chapter are more like parables. They do not seem to have clear meanings but will provide comfort as they unfold and begin to make sense.

Notice that the Bible says in Matthew 24:25, "See, I have told you beforehand." Notice the first word of this verse. The word see is present tense. Sometimes a prophecy may not reveal itself until sometime later on. All of these prophecies have one thing in common. They always bring us to a good place.

A prophecy has to line up with the Word of God. A prophecy of the New Testament will never condemn or judge (John 3:17). A prophecy will be an encouragement and will always produce good fruit.

The Holy Spirit comes upon a believer to make available the power to heal, perform miracles, and prophesy. These gifts are to aid the church as well as attract people into the kingdom of God. These ministries provide people with an ability to stand stronger (longsuffering). They are an act of gentleness and will lead people to something good.

The Holy Spirit can simply fall on you during a church service or personal time when learning about God's Word. The Bible tells us in Acts 10:44, "While Peter was still speaking these words, the Holy Spirit fell upon all those who heard the word."

Another way to receive the baptism of the Holy Spirit is to have someone lay hands on you and ask for it. In Acts 19:6, we read, "And when Paul had laid hands on them, the Holy Spirit came upon them."

In conclusion, the Spirit on the outside gives us these three gifts:

Gifts	Fruit
Healing Miracles Prophecy	Longsuffering Gentleness Goodness

Chapter Six

Access

And when Paul had laid hands on them, the Holy
Spirit came upon them, and they spoke with tongues
and prophesied.

—Acts 19:6

6

Access

The Birth of Levi[19]

"This time my Husband will become attached to me," she said, "so I will name him Levi." She did not know the significance of what she said. Some 430 years later, the family of Levi would be attached as the caretakers of the tabernacle. The Levites were throughout the tabernacle, much like the Holy Spirit can be throughout us.

The Levites were to camp around the tabernacle. They would be responsible for all set up of the tabernacle. If the Israelites were to move, the Levites were responsible for moving the tabernacle. Levites also provided all tabernacle maintenance, inside and out.

Selected priests came from the tribe of Levi. Once selected, a priest had to have anointing oil poured on his head. Only a priest who had this done could access the most holy place inside of the tabernacle. In this most holy place, the priest would receive a word from God. The priest would take the word and release it to those outside of the tabernacle. The access to the inside of the tabernacle brought the Word of God to the outside. This word of God was the Spirit of God.

The Bible tells us that the Levites also protected the children of God from wrath. The Levites were not included in the census that counted all the men fit for battle; the Levites provided protection not by might but by the Spirit of God.

---

[19] Supporting Scriptures pages 105–06.

In this chapter, we will look at the remaining three gifts of the Spirit. These gifts connect our natural outward selves to our supernatural God inside of us. We will study the tabernacle to learn the principles of discernment, tongues, and interpretation of tongues. These are the last of the gifts listed in 1 Corinthians 12:10.

Near the beginning of chapter five, we looked at Luke 4:1. Luke says, "Then Jesus, being filled with the Holy Spirit . . ." We learned that the word translated as "filled" comes from a Greek word pronounced "play'-race." This word means, "Well supplied, filled and covered over."

When we receive the gift of salvation, the Holy Spirit automatically takes up residence inside of us. We are immediately born again or born of the Spirit. The next level for a believer is to receive baptism in the Holy Spirit.

When you receive baptism in the Holy Spirit, you receive an anointing with oil. This is what happened to Jesus when He received His water baptism in the Jordan. The Bible says in Luke 3:22, "And the Holy Spirit descended in bodily form like a dove upon Him." This was His anointing as a priest.

Jesus said in Luke 4:18, "The Spirit of the Lord is upon Me, Because He has anointed Me To preach the gospel to the poor; He has sent Me to heal the brokenhearted, To proclaim liberty to the captives And recovery of sight to the blind, To set at liberty those who are oppressed."

The Holy Spirit anointed Jesus as a priest to minister to the people. In this same way, the Holy Spirit anoints you as a priest when He comes upon you. You then have access to the most holy place. These remaining gifts are a means to access the most holy place.

The Bible tells us in Acts 10:45-46, "The Jewish believers who came with Peter were amazed that the gift of the Holy Spirit had been poured out on the Gentiles, too. For they heard them speaking in tongues and praising God" (NLT). When the Jewish believers saw that the gentiles were speaking in tongues, they knew that the Holy Spirit had fallen upon them.

Study the illustration on the following page, and take notice of the three entrances that take you to the most holy place.

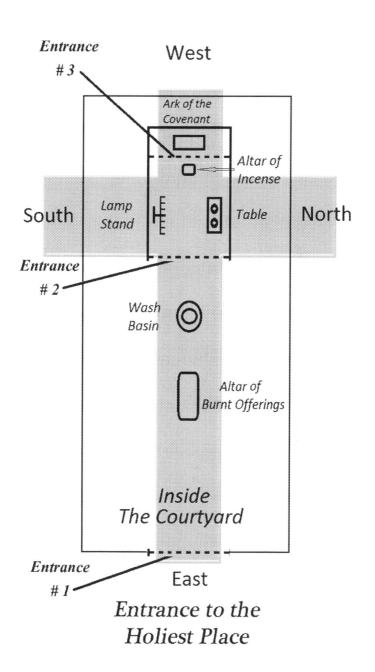

Entrance
3

West

Ark of the
Covenant

Altar of
Incense

South

Lamp
Stand

Table

North

Entrance
2

Wash
Basin

Altar of
Burnt Offerings

*Inside
The Courtyard*

Entrance
1

East

Entrance to the
Holiest Place

These three entrances bring you from the bottom of the cross to the highest place. This is the place of our God most high. You may also see this as an entrance from the outside into the very heart of God. I did a quick search on the internet for synonyms of the word entrance. I made an interesting discovery. According to Thesaurus.com, the word baptism is a synonym of entrance.

When the Holy Spirit has baptized you, you receive the benefit of being able to enter into the most holy place. Each entrance is a privilege. Each privilege is a gift. You are baptized in the Spirit when He comes upon you.

The First Entrance—Discernment

The first entrance brings us into the courtyard. This would be the gift of discernment. The word discernment means judgment.[20] The sin offerings took place in the courtyard. God's people transferred their sin onto innocent animals and then judged the animals on the altar.

To take full advantage of this gift, you must know that Jesus was your sin offering. We need to be completely conscious of the flawless offering provided by Jesus. The more we grasp the perfection of His offering, the more powerful our faith will be as we enter into the tabernacle.

It is impossible to take full advantage of entering into the tabernacle without the faith produced by the gift of discernment.

The Second Entrance—Tongues

The next gift is praying in tongues. It is an action of faith. It is among the highest levels of prayer before God. Inside of the tabernacle is the altar of incense. The Bible says in Revelation 5:8,

---

[20]   http://dictionary.reference.com/browse/discernment.

"Golden bowls full of incense, which are the prayers of the saints." Inside the tabernacle, our prayers are as incense to God. We are inside the tabernacle when we pray in tongues.

The apostle Paul wrote in Romans 8:26, "The Spirit also helps in our weaknesses. For we do not know what we should pray for as we ought, but the Spirit Himself makes intercession for us with groanings which cannot be uttered." Take hold of this. The Holy Spirit, the breath of God, prays for us when we do not know how to pray for ourselves.

Tongues are a language that takes place in the spirit realm. Notice that Paul said that intercession took place with "groanings that cannot be uttered." The original Greek uses a single word that means *unspeakable*. In English, we read, *cannot be uttered.*[21] In other words, these groanings cannot be spoken. The Bible says in 1 Corinthians 14:2, "For he who speaks in a tongue does not speak to men but to God, for no one understands *him;* however, in the spirit he speaks mysteries."

When we pray in tongues, we are exercising the action of faith. The communication is actually taking place in the spirit realm. It has nothing to do with the sound we hear in the natural. There is a misleading notion that as you mature, you must produce a greater vocabulary of noises when you pray in tongues. Some people do, but I never have.

This belief held me back for years. I had a wonderful gift that I did not use. I am not one of those people who can produce a variety of new noises every time I pray. One way is no more powerful than the other is. Either way, you have the full power of the Holy Spirit interceding for you when you pray in tongues. In fact, you have the Spirit without measure praying for you.

There are four major fixtures inside the tabernacle. First there is the ark of the covenant in the most holy place. Next there is the altar of incense, the table, and the lampstand in the

---

[21]   James Strong, *Strong's Talking Greek and Hebrew Dictionary* (Austin, TX: Wordsearch Corp., 2002), Bible study software, Strong's number, G215.

holy place, outside of the curtain. In Exodus 25:10-30, we find the measurements for the ark of the covenant and the table. In Exodus 30:2, we find the measurements for the altar of incense. The measurements for the lampstand are not found anywhere in the Scriptures. In other words, the Spirit (lampstand) is without measure inside the tabernacle. When you pray in tongues, you are tapping into the full power of the Holy Spirit.

Many believers do not understand the gift of tongues. Recently, at the church I attend, we had an altar call for people who wanted to receive baptism in the Spirit. I sometimes assist in praying for people at the front. I prayed over about a half dozen people. All except one of the people I prayed for already had the Holy Spirit on them. They just did not know it.

I have been a Christian about twenty-three years. The first time I prayed in tongues was about seventeen years ago. Just like so many people, I was never sure if I ever received baptism in the Spirit. This confidence only came about three years ago. I finally decided that I had to have been baptized in the Spirit. I was just going to believe that it was so. I just said the same string of five or six syllables repeatedly. These are the same syllables I had had for fourteen years. I felt foolish, so I did it in private.

Every teaching on tongues will tell you that you have to receive this gift by faith. In faith, I expected something to happen. I prayed in tongues whenever I had the chance, and things started to happen.

Amazing things took place. On some occasions, I have had visions. At other times I have received revelations. Bad habits have even started to fade away. Sometimes I just feel very encouraged. I always expect something good to happen.

I have come to realize that praying in tongues is a faith mode. The sounds that come out of us are completely meaningless. It makes no difference how many or how creative the sounds might be. It is the faith that moves the Holy Spirit to pray.

I love to start my day in prayer. I have always enjoyed praying. God has blessed me with a wonderful desire to do it as much as possible. God has heavily armed me with Scripture that comes out when I pray. If you want to sense power in prayer, just speak God's Word in prayer.

One morning when I was about to pray, the Lord said to me, "I want you to only pray in tongues today. I want you to have the same faith in tongues as you do in My Word." This was a wonderful revelation to me. Whether I pray the Word of God or pray in the Holy Spirit, I am praying with the full power of God.

Every time I pray in tongues, it is an exercise in faith. Just like exercising my body, over time my faith gets stronger. In Jude 1:20 the Bible tells us, "But you, beloved, building yourselves up on your most holy faith, praying in the Holy Spirit." This makes it clear. Pray in tongues and build yourself up on faith. This is not just any faith; it is the most holy faith that comes from God.

The Holy Spirit is our helper. We have to do something for Him to help. When we pray in tongues, we operate in faith. Faith always moves the Spirit.

If you believe that the Spirit has fallen on you at some time, then just fashion a sound. It can be any sound you find easy to make so you do not have to concentrate on it. Just keep repeating it. If you believe that you are praying in tongues, then you are.

I know that many people have had some incredible experience when they first prayed in tongues, but most people do not. For the first eighteen years that I was Christian, I never took advantage of this wonderful gift because I was not sure if I even had it.

The Bible says in Ephesians 6:18, "Pray in the Spirit at all times and on every occasion. Stay alert and be persistent in your prayers for all believers everywhere" (NLT). When we pray, we can be praying for believers everywhere.

I have on occasion even woken up during the night and felt led to pray in the Spirit. The Spirit works through man. Man releases the power of God by faith. We take action. The action is faith. This allows the Holy Spirit to intercede in the spirit realm.

The Holy Spirit will sometimes find a willing person who will pray in tongues. I always enjoy when the Holy Spirit selects me. I have become very easy to impose upon for God. When you are easy to impose upon, the Bible says that you are meek.

It seems that praying in the Spirit has produced the fruit of meekness in me.

I always get refreshed praying in the Spirit, even if I miss some sleep. Meekness means being easily imposed upon. When I wake up for the Holy Spirit and pray, it is a demonstration of meekness toward the Holy Spirit.

If you want God to work through you, pray in the Spirit. This will make it easy for Him to impose upon you. The Bible says in 1 Corinthians 15:58, "Knowing that your labor is not in vain in the Lord." He always makes it worth your while.

The first entrance of discernment produces the fruit of faith. This second entrance of tongues makes it easy for God to impose upon you. The gift of tongues produces the fruit of meekness. Who knows—maybe God will use you to write books or invent something.

The Third Entrance—Interpretation of Tongues

This is the last of the nine gifts. This is the entrance into the most holy place. This gift is available to every believer who has passed through the second entrance. Paul wrote in 1 Corinthians 14:13, "Therefore let him who speaks in a tongue pray that he may interpret." This is a place of powerful communion with God.

When you enter into the most holy place, you receive revelation from God. Whenever I pray in tongues, something happens. I will typically feel refreshed and encouraged. I usually get clarification on something, and I have even received visions.

Tongues are a supernatural language that takes place in the spirit realm. It is literally the Holy Spirit praying on our behalf. When we pray in tongues, we get refreshed. This is when the Holy Spirit ministers to us. In these situations, we want to have revelation on what He is saying. I have often received an answer to a question that I have had, or sometimes I get a leading to do something.

This is the gift of interpretation of tongues. In these moments, the Lord delivered me from smoking. When I was ready, He told me what I needed to do. It was a personal plan just for me. In my case, this was an impossible goal for me to reach on my own. When the Holy Spirit gives you self-control, there is no considerable effort on your part.

There are times when I pray in tongues that I may not sense much of anything. Whenever this happens, I know I am going to receive a wonderful word of encouragement. Sometimes it can take up to a day to receive an interpretation of tongues. If I do not feel encouraged and edified, I know I will receive an interpretation. Something always happens when I pray in tongues.

When you enter into this most holy place, bondages are broken. I smoked cigarettes and cigars for about thirty-five years. I tried everything possible to quit. I finally gave up on trying. Shortly after I started praying in tongues, I talked to God about it.

Because of praying in tongues, I was getting instructions through interpretation that prompted me to quit. The Holy Spirit helped in my weakness (Rom. 8:26), and God prompted me when I was ready to quit. I have received complete freedom from that bondage. This gift provides the fruit of self-control.

Discernment produces faith, tongues produce meekness, and interpretation of tongues produces self-control.

Gifts	Fruit
Discernment Tongues Interpretation	Faith Meekness Self-control

Chapter Seven

The Body

For as the body is one and has many members, but
all the members of that one body, being many, are
one body, so also is Christ.

—1 Corinthians 12:12

7

The Body

The Perfume Maker[22]

He begins with a mixture of oils and ground up spices, nearly forty pounds in all. He starts with a double portion of oil pressed from resin found in myrrh bark. He then takes a single portion of sweet-smelling cinnamon, finely ground and beaten into powder as fine as dust. The perfume maker then adds a single portion of sweet-smelling cane oil that has been beaten and pressed from cane trees. The last fragrant element is a double portion of cassia bark. The bark has also been finely ground and beaten into powder, the same way as the cinnamon.

The perfume maker takes these four fragrances and measures them by weight. He mixes them with one gallon of pure olive oil, producing a substance ordained by God. This is a special mixture of anointing oil fashioned as God has requested. It will produce holiness in all that it touches. This anointing oil is for every item used in the tabernacle. This oil anoints the priests who enter into the tabernacle as well.

The Ingredients

We have already understood that the olive oil is a sign of the Holy Spirit. Looking a little deeper, we can see that the four

---

[22]   Supporting Scriptures page 107.

fragrances reveal Jesus. The Bible says in Ephesians 5:2 that Jesus is "an offering and a sacrifice to God for a sweet-smelling aroma." This says that Jesus is a sweet-smelling aroma. These fragrant spices have been pressed and beaten from trees. This was prophetic of Jesus, who was bruised and beaten on the cross (Isa. 53:5). This mixture included the sacrifice of Jesus—four fragrances—and the Holy Spirit—olive oil.

Psalm 133

Psalm 133:1-3 says:

> How wonderful and pleasant it is when brothers live together in harmony! For harmony is as precious as the anointing oil that was poured over Aaron's head, that ran down his beard and onto the border of his robe. Harmony is as refreshing as the dew from Mount Hermon that falls on the mountains of Zion. And there the Lord has pronounced his blessing, even life everlasting (NLT).

This Psalm has been one of my favorite Psalms for a long time. I have always liked verse 1, which says, "How wonderful and pleasant it is when brothers live together in harmony!" I also like the last verse, which says, "And there the Lord has pronounced his blessing, even life everlasting." Of course, the Psalm is not complete without verse 2. Verse 2 gives us an understanding of how the body comes together.

This Psalm is prophetic of the body of Christ. When we dig in to verse two, this is what we find. The precious oil, of course, is a mixture of the Holy Spirit and Christ crucified. This oil starts upon the head and runs down the beard of Aaron. According to *Hitchcock's Dictionary of Bible Names*[23], the name Aaron means teacher, high up, a mountain of strength. This makes it clear that the head is Jesus. The oil runs down from the head to the beard. The word beard in the Old Testament comes from a Hebrew word that means mature or aged[24]. The oil then continues right down to the border of his robe.

The first verse discusses brothers living together in harmony and therefore gives us an indication that this Psalm is about the church body. Verse 2 confirms it by revealing that the oil starts with our Teacher in a high place, who is a mountain of strength. The oil then runs on to the mature in Christ and then to the rest of the body. Now verse 3 tells us that the blessing is in the body when we are in unity.

Notice that this anointing starts with the mature in Christ. This is not the same as the individual anointing that is available to everyone who is born of the Spirit. To have a ministry in any of these gifts, you need to be close to the Head, Jesus Christ. This means you spend time with Him and in His Word.

In the same way the Holy Spirit fills, comes upon, and saturates an individual believer, the Holy Spirit fills, comes upon, and saturates the body of Christ. Each gift is an office of ministry in the body of Christ. The apostle Paul told us in 1 Corinthians 12:5, "There are differences of ministries, but the same Lord."

Paul then went on to say in verse 11, "But one and the same Spirit works all these things, distributing to each one individually as He wills." This is to say that each ministry will operate through an individual person as a member of the body. Let us look at these offices of ministry.

---

[23] Roswell D. Hitchcock, *Hitchcock's Bible Names Dictionary* (Austin, TX: Wordsearch Corp, 2002) Bible study software.

[24] James Strong, *Strong's Talking Greek and Hebrew Dictionary* (Austin, TX: Wordsearch Corp., 2002), Bible study software, Strong's number, H2206.

The first three gifts are automatically available to every church that believes Jesus Christ is the only way of salvation for humankind. God will put wisdom, knowledge, and faith in each church. This way the church will be a source of love, joy, and peace. We simply pray for these gifts regularly as if they are our daily bread.

The Holy Spirit distributes these gifts as He wills. Typically, these gifts operate very subtly. At times, a person operating in these ministries may not even realize it.

Wisdom	Love
Knowledge	Joy
Faith	Peace

It is important for us to seek out the presence of these gifts because they are the foundation of maturity and growth for our church. We should ask just as Paul did when he prayed for the church of Ephesus.

Paul said in Ephesians 1:16-17, "*I do not cease to give thanks for you, making mention of you in my prayers: that the God of our Lord Jesus Christ, the Father of glory, may give to you the spirit of wisdom and revelation in the knowledge of Him.*" Without ceasing, Paul was praying for this church to receive wisdom and knowledge. Then in chapter 3, he prayed for this church to have faith (v. 17).

The Holy Spirit often gives these next three offices to those in a position to spread the Word. It is quite common for a preacher of the Word to have one of these offices.

```
┌─────────────────────┐   ┌─────────────────────┐
│      Healing        │   │   Longsuffering     │
│                     │   │                     │
│      Miracles       │   │    Gentleness       │
│                     │   │                     │
│      Prophecy       │   │     Goodness        │
└─────────────────────┘   └─────────────────────┘
```

These ministry gifts also operate as the Spirit wills. The Bible says in Hebrews 2:4, "And God confirmed the message by giving signs and wonders and various miracles and gifts of the Holy Spirit whenever he chose" (NLT). You are more likely to see these offices operating during a church service to confirm the presence of God.

There is a difference between the personal gifts you receive as an individual and these offices. These offices are a much more powerful manifestation of the Spirit. They can provide the church with gifts of healing, miracles, or prophecy to a multitude of people at a single event. The Holy Spirit needs to lead these events.

Healings, miracles, and prophecy not only strengthen and encourage believers; they also tend to be the front-page news that attracts the unsaved. These gifts are to provide health and *growth* to the body of Christ. The fruits of longsuffering (power to stand), kind acts, and goodness accomplish exactly that.

The Holy Spirit provides these last three offices to build strength and maturity into the church.

```
┌─────────────────────┐   ┌─────────────────────┐
│    Discernment      │   │       Faith         │
│                     │   │                     │
│      Tongues        │   │     Meekness        │
│                     │   │                     │
│   Interpretation    │   │    Self-control     │
└─────────────────────┘   └─────────────────────┘
```

These ministry offices are the direct link of two-way communications between God and the church. Discernment is to expose deceptions of the enemy, tongues is the supernatural language of the spirit realm, and interpretation of tongues defines the natural translation of this supernatural language.

The purpose behind each gift is to produce fruit. Wisdom has no value unless it produces love; knowledge has no value unless it produces joy and so on.

Love, Joy, and Peace

We know that Jesus operated in the first three offices because of the fruit He produced in the church. First John 4:19 tells us, "We love Him because He first loved us." Love comes from the ministry of wisdom. Luke 10:17 says, "Then the seventy returned with joy." The knowledge of the authority Jesus gave them created joy. The fruit that comes from faith is peace. Jesus said in John 14:27, "Peace I leave with you, My peace I give to you; not as the world gives do I give to you . . ." This came to us because he provided the body with a greater faith (Heb. 11:40).

Longsuffering, Gentleness, and Goodness

We also know that Jesus operated in the offices of healing, miracles, and prophecy (Matt. 8, 25, Luke 5). The gospels are full of examples of these gifts ministered by Jesus. The Bible also gives plenty of reports about people who were motivated to be kind to others and do good things as a result. Unfortunately, many people wrongfully believe that this is the way to heaven. Receiving the gift of salvation that was provided by the sacrifice of Jesus is the only way to heaven. Being kind to others and doing good things are fruit that comes naturally because of these gifts of the Holy Spirit being manifest.

Faith, Meekness, and Self-Control

The fruits of the remaining offices are faith, meekness, and self-control. You may be familiar with the account of Jesus walking on water. You may also be aware that the apostle Peter walked on water too.

The Bible tells us in Matthew 14:28 that Peter said to Jesus, "Lord, if it is You, command me to come to You on the water." Peter was not convinced he was seeing Jesus.

The gift of discernment was in operation here. Discernment is more powerful than simple words. The words of Jesus had the power of discernment in them. They produced enough faith in Peter that he actually walked on the water (Matt. 14:29). The next two offices go hand in hand. These are tongues and interpretation of tongues.

We saw earlier that Jesus had the Spirit without limit. We also learned that Jesus spoke God's words (John 3:34). There is no indication that Jesus ministered in tongues. Since Jesus spoke the Father's words, the Father literally spoke through Him. The ministry of tongues would not have been necessary. However, His ministry did produce the fruit of meekness.

Meekness is a yielding to God and allowing Him to impose on you. Meekness was a fruit of Jesus's ministry. A clear example of this was a tax collector named Zacchaeus. The Bible tells us in Luke 19:8 that he put on a dinner for Jesus. There was also the man delivered from demons in Mark 5:18. He wanted to join Jesus in His ministry. In both situations, these men yielded themselves to Jesus.

Jesus also provided self-control. This too would have been supernatural since it is impossible for man to stop sinning in the natural. Man needs the power of God to stop sinning. There was the woman caught in adultery and the man who received healing for an infirmity that plagued him for thirty-eight years. Jesus told these people to sin no more (John 8:11, 5:14). He would not have told them to do something without empowering them to do it.

In this chapter, we realized that an individual believer is empowered with the same gifts as the entire body of Christ. However, the body of Christ receives these gifts without measure. As an individual believer, discover how to tap into the gifts that produce the fruit. We are going to discuss this in the next chapter.

Chapter Eight

Take Advantage

I returned and saw under the sun that—The race is not to the swift, Nor the battle to the strong, Nor bread to the wise, Nor riches to men of understanding, Nor favor to men of skill.

—Ecclesiastes 9:11

Take Advantage

Continually

The Bible says in Leviticus 24:2, "Command the children of Israel that they bring to you pure oil of pressed olives for the light, to make the lamps burn continually." If you read verse 3, the priest would only light the lamp at night. That means that there should be another comma after the word burn and before the word continually.

In other words, they were supposed to *collect the oil for the lamps continually*. That was confirmed when Jesus said in the Lord's Prayer, "Give us this day our daily bread" (Matt. 6:11). By asking continually, we never forget that He is our source.

God has provided these gifts to us for a reason. Jesus told us in John 15:16-17, "You did not choose Me, but I chose you and appointed you that you should go and bear fruit, and *that* your fruit should remain, that whatever you ask the Father in My name He may give you. These things I command you, that you love one another." Notice He said, "That you love one another." The reason for the fruit is so that we love one another.

The Personal Gifts

The gifts cause fruit to overflow from us. The fruit is a tool for us to love one another. If we understand this, then we realize that God wants us to have these gifts. What could we do to restrict the flow of these gifts through our lives?

When God led me to write these books, I wondered why He would have me do it. In the church I attend, there are so many better and more qualified people to do it. Then I heard in my thoughts, *Because you know what you are without Me.* I know that I could not possibly do anything worthwhile without Him.

When we know that we need God's strength to do something, it opens the door for God to move on our behalf. I love how the Message translation of the Bible puts it. In 2 Corinthians 12:10, the apostle Paul said, "Now I take limitations in stride, and with good cheer, these limitations that cut me down to size—abuse, accidents, opposition, bad breaks. I just let Christ take over! And so the weaker I get, the stronger I become."

King Solomon said in Ecclesiastes 9:11, "I returned and saw under the sun that—The race *is* not to the swift, Nor the battle to the strong, Nor bread to the wise, Nor riches to men of understanding, Nor favor to men of skill; But time and chance happen to them all." Notice that he said that time and chance happen to all. You do not need any special skills to win the battle. All that you need is the Holy Spirit.

These gifts are available to all. If you think God will not use you, then think about the talking donkey in Numbers 22:30. If you think God would not talk to you because you are not good enough, then think about Cain. Right after Cain murdered his brother Abel, God talked with him (Gen, 4:8-9).

The only obstacle to receiving these gifts is believing there is some reason you cannot have them.

Gifts that Become an Office

These gifts can sometimes be an office for a believer. A pastor may have the office of healing, or an elder in the church may have the office of discernment or tongues. The Bible tells us in 1 Corinthians 12:11, "But one and the same Spirit works all these things, distributing to each one individually as He wills."

By taking advantage of the personal gifts available to us, we can learn our purpose for the body of Christ. The apostle Paul tells us in 1 Corinthians 12:23, "And the parts we regard as less honorable are those we clothe with the greatest care. So we carefully protect those parts that should not be seen" (NLT).

Whatever your role in the ministry is, whether it is apparent to others or not, you deserve to be honored. You are a child of God, and He has a purpose for you to fulfill.

When you discover your purpose for the kingdom of God, you will overflow in the fruit of the Holy Spirit. You will experience a life worth living. I have included the illustration on the following page for your reference.

Remind yourself regularly what God has made available to every believer, and continually ask for these gifts in prayer.

Gifts of the Spirit   *Fruit of the Spirit*
1 Cor. 12:8–10   *Gal. 5:22-23*

Wisdom Knowledge Faith	Love Joy Peace
Healing Miracles Prophecy	Longsuffering Gentleness Goodness
Discernment Tongues Interpretation	Faith Meekness Self-control

Appendix A

Chapter 1—The Tabernacle

Build Me a Tabernacle

Exodus, chapters 1-19, 24, and 25 where the foundation for the Hollywood motion picture titled, *The Ten Commandments.*

Exodus 24:12, "Then the Lord said to Moses, "Come up to me on the mountain. Stay there, and I will give you the tablets of stone on which I have inscribed the instructions and commands so you can teach the people" (NLT).

Exodus 24:18, "Then Moses disappeared into the cloud as he climbed higher up the mountain. He remained on the mountain forty days and forty nights" (NLT).

Exodus 25:9, "You must build this Tabernacle and its furnishings exactly according to the pattern I will show you" (NLT).

The Grand Tour

Exodus 27:18, "So the entire courtyard will be 150 feet long and 75 feet wide, with curtain walls 71/2 feet high, made from finely woven linen. The bases for the posts will be made of bronze." (NLT).

Exodus 27:16, "For the entrance to the courtyard, make a curtain that is 30 feet long. Make it from finely woven linen, and decorate it with beautiful embroidery in blue, purple, and scarlet thread. Support it with four posts, each securely set in its own base" (NLT).

Exodus 27:13, "The east end of the courtyard, the front, will also be 75 feet long" (NLT).

Exodus 29:38-39, "These are the sacrifices you are to offer regularly on the altar. Each day, offer two lambs that are a year old, one in the morning and the other in the evening" (NLT).

Exodus 29:40-41, "With one of them, offer two quarts of choice flour mixed with one quart of pure oil of pressed olives; also, offer one quart of wine as a liquid offering. Offer the other lamb in the evening, along with the same offerings of flour and wine as in the morning. It will be a pleasing aroma, a special gift presented to the Lord" (NLT).

Exodus 29:35-36, "This is how you will ordain Aaron and his sons to their offices, just as I have commanded you. The ordination ceremony will go on for seven days. Each day you must sacrifice a young bull as a sin offering to purify them, making them right with the Lord. Afterward, cleanse the altar by purifying it; make it holy by anointing it with oil" (NLT).

Exodus 27:1-2, "Using acacia wood, construct a square altar 71/2 feet wide, 71/2 feet long, and 41/2 feet high. Make horns for each of its four corners so that the horns and altar are all one piece. Overlay the altar with bronze" (NLT).

Exodus 30:18-20, "Make a bronze washbasin with a bronze stand. Place it between the Tabernacle and the altar, and fill it with water. Aaron and his sons will wash their hands and feet there. They must wash with water whenever they go into the Tabernacle to appear before the Lord and when they approach the altar to burn up their special gifts to the Lord—or they will die!" (NLT).

Exodus 26:14, "Complete the tent covering with a protective layer of tanned ram skins and a layer of fine goatskin leather" (NLT).

Exodus 26:36, "Make another curtain for the entrance to the sacred tent. Make it of finely woven linen and embroider it with exquisite designs, using blue, purple, and scarlet thread" (NLT).

Exodus 26:15-16, "For the framework of the Tabernacle, construct frames of acacia wood. Each frame must be 15 feet high and 27-inches wide" (NLT).

Exodus 26:18, "Make twenty of these frames to support the curtains on the south side of the Tabernacle" (NLT).

Exodus 26:20, "For the north side of the Tabernacle, make another twenty frames" (NLT).

Exodus 26:25, "So there will be eight frames at the rear of the Tabernacle, set in sixteen silver bases—two bases under each frame" (NLT).

Exodus 26:29, "Overlay the frames with gold, and make gold rings to hold the crossbars. Overlay the crossbars with gold as well" (NLT).

Exodus 25:23-25, "Then make a table of acacia wood, 36-inches long, 18-inches wide, and 27-inches high. Overlay it with pure gold and run a gold molding around the edge. Decorate it with a 3-inch border all around, and run a gold molding along the border" (NLT).

Exodus 25:29-30, "Make special containers of pure gold for the table—bowls, pans, pitchers, and jars—to be used in pouring out liquid offerings. Place the Bread of the Presence on the table to remain before me at all times" (NLT).

Leviticus 24:5-7, "And you shall take fine flour and bake twelve cakes with it; two-tenths of an ephah shall be in each cake [of the showbread or bread of the Presence]. And you shall set them in two rows, six in a row, upon the table of pure gold before the Lord. You shall put pure frankincense [in a bowl or spoon] beside each row that it may be with the bread as a memorial portion, an offering to be made by fire to the Lord" (AMP).

Exodus 26:35, "Place the table outside the inner curtain on the north side of the Tabernacle, and place the lampstand across the room on the south side" (NLT).

Exodus 25:31-32, "Make a lampstand of pure, hammered gold. Make the entire lampstand and its decorations of one piece—the base, center stem, lamp cups, buds, and petals. make it with six branches going out from the center stem, three on each side" (NLT).

Exodus 25:37, "Then make the seven lamps for the lampstand, and set them so they reflect their light forward" (NLT).

Exodus 25:39, "You will need seventy-five pounds of pure gold for the lampstand and its accessories" (NLT).

Exodus 26:31, "For the inside of the Tabernacle, make a special curtain of finely woven linen. Decorate it with blue, purple, and scarlet thread and with skillfully embroidered cherubim" (NLT).

Leviticus 6:16, "And the remainder of it Aaron and his sons shall eat; with unleavened bread it shall be eaten in a holy place; in the court of the tabernacle of meeting they shall eat it" (NKJV).

Exodus 26:33, "Hang the inner curtain from clasps, and put the Ark of the Covenant in the room behind it. This curtain will separate the Holy Place from the Most Holy Place" (NLT).

Exodus 30:6, "Place the incense altar just outside the inner curtain that shields the Ark of the Covenant, in front of the Ark's cover—the place of atonement—that covers the tablets inscribed with the terms of the covenant. I will meet with you there" (NLT).

Exodus 30:1-3, "Then make another altar of acacia wood for burning incense. Make it 18-inches square and 36-inches high, with horns at the corners carved from the same piece of wood as the altar itself. Overlay the top, sides, and horns of the altar with pure gold, and run a gold molding around the entire altar" (NLT).

Exodus 25:10-11, "Have the people make an Ark of acacia wood—a sacred chest 45-inches long, 27-inches wide, and 27-inches high. Overlay it inside and outside with pure gold, and run a molding of gold all around it" (NLT).

Exodus 25:16, "When the Ark is finished, place inside it the stone tablets inscribed with the terms of the covenant, which I will give to you." (NLT).

Exodus 25:17-20, "Then make the Ark's cover—the place of atonement—from pure gold. It must be 45-inches long and 27-inches wide. Then make two cherubim from hammered gold, and place them on the two ends of the atonement cover. Mold the cherubim on each end of the atonement cover, making it all of one piece of gold. The cherubim will face each other and look down on the atonement cover. With their wings spread above it, they will protect it" (NLT).

Exodus 25:22, "I will meet with you there and talk to you from above the atonement cover between the gold cherubim that hover over the Ark of the Covenant. From there I will give you my commands people of Israel" (NLT).

Revelation 22:5, "And there will be no night there—no need for lamps or sun—for the Lord God will shine on them" (NLT).

Exodus 33:20, "But you may not look directly at my face, for no one may see me and live" (NLT).

Exodus 25:8, "Have the people of Israel build me a holy sanctuary so I can live among them" (NLT).

Appendix B

Chapter 2—Who is the Holy Spirit?

Let's Talk

John 13:1-2, "Before the Passover celebration, Jesus knew that his hour had come to leave this world and return to his Father. He had loved his disciples during his ministry on earth, and now he loved them to the very end. It was time for supper, and the devil had already prompted Judas, son of Simon Iscariot, to betray Jesus" (NLT).

John 13:7, "Jesus replied, "You don't understand now what I am doing, but someday you will" (NLT).

John 13:27, "When Judas had eaten the bread, Satan entered into him. Then Jesus told him, "Hurry and do what you're going to do" (NLT).

John 14:7, "If you had really known me, you would know who my Father is. From now on, you do know him and have seen him!" (NLT).

John 14:8, "Philip said, "Lord, show us the Father, and we will be satisfied" (NLT).

John 14:10, "Don't you believe that I am in the Father and the Father is in me? The words I speak are not my own, but my Father who lives in me does his work through me." (NLT).

John 14:26, "But when the Father sends the Advocate as my representative—that is, the Holy Spirit—he will teach you everything and will remind you of everything I have told you" (NLT).

Exodus 33:22, "As my glorious presence passes by, I will hide you in the crevice of the rock and cover you with my hand until I have passed by" (NLT).

John 1:1, "In the beginning the Word already existed. The Word was with God, and the Word was God" (NLT).

John 1:14, "So the Word became human and made his home among us. He was full of unfailing love and faithfulness. And we have seen his glory, the glory of the Father's one and only Son" (NLT).

Genesis 2:7, "Then the Lord God formed the man from the dust of the ground. He breathed the breath of life into the man's nostrils, and the man became a living person" (NLT).

John 3:8, "The wind blows (breathes) where it wills; and though you hear its sound, yet you neither know where it comes from nor where it is going. So it is with everyone who is born of the Spirit" (AMP).

Appendix C

Chapter 3—The Holy Spirit and the Tabernacle

The Secret Meeting

John 2:9, "When the master of ceremonies tasted the water that was now wine, not knowing where it had come from (though, of course, the servants knew), he called the bridegroom over" (NLT).

John 2:23, "Now when he was in Jerusalem at the Passover, in the feast day, many believed in his name, when they saw the miracles which he did" (KJV).

Exodus 13:9-10, "This annual festival will be a visible sign to you, like a mark branded on your hand or your forehead. Let it remind you always to recite this teaching of the Lord: 'With a strong hand, the Lord rescued you from Egypt.' So observe the decree of this festival at the appointed time each year" (NLT).

John 3:1-2, "There was a man named Nicodemus, a Jewish religious leader who was a Pharisee. After dark one evening, he came to speak with Jesus. "Rabbi," he said, "we all know that God has sent you to teach us. Your miraculous signs are evidence that God is with you" (NLT).

Matthew 8:16, "That evening many demon-possessed people were brought to Jesus. He cast out the evil spirits with a simple command, and he healed all the sick" (NLT).

Matthew 8:2-3, "Suddenly, a man with leprosy approached him and knelt before him. "Lord," the man said, "if you are willing, you can heal me and make me clean." Jesus reached out and touched him. "I am willing," he said. "Be healed!" And instantly the leprosy disappeared" (NLT).

Luke 4:27, "And there were many lepers in Israel in the time of the prophet Elisha, but the only one healed was Naaman, a Syrian" (NLT).

John 3:3, "Jesus replied, "I tell you the truth, unless you are born again, you cannot see the Kingdom of God" (NLT).

John 3:5, "Jesus replied, "I assure you, no one can enter the Kingdom of God without being born of water and the Spirit" (NLT).

1 Peter 3:20, "those who disobeyed God long ago when God waited patiently while Noah was building his boat. Only eight people were saved from drowning in that terrible flood" (NLT).

1 Peter 2:24, "He personally carried our sins in his body on the cross so that we can be dead to sin and live for what is right. By his wounds you are healed" (NLT).

Hebrews 10:12, "But our High Priest [Jesus] offered himself to God as a single sacrifice for sins, good for all time. Then he sat down in the place of honor at God's right hand" (NLT).

Hebrews 10:14, "For by one offering he hath perfected for ever them that are sanctified" (KJV).

Appendix D

Chapter 4—Three Cups

Filling the Cups

Exodus 29:38-39, "These are the sacrifices you are to offer regularly on the altar. Each day, offer two lambs that are a year old, one in the morning and the other in the evening" (NLT).

1 Samuel 3:15, "Samuel stayed in bed until morning, then got up and opened the doors of the Tabernacle as usual" (NLT).

Exodus 30:7-8, "Every morning when Aaron maintains the lamps, he must burn fragrant incense on the altar. And each evening when he lights the lamps, he must again burn incense in the Lord's presence. This must be done from generation to generation" (NLT).

Exodus 27:21, "The lampstand will stand in the Tabernacle, in front of the inner curtain that shields the Ark of the Covenant. Aaron and his sons must keep the lamps burning in the Lord's presence all night" (NLT).

Exodus 30:25-27, "Like a skilled incense maker, blend these ingredients to make a holy anointing oil. Use this sacred oil to anoint the Tabernacle, the Ark of the Covenant, the table and all its utensils, the lampstand and all its accessories, the incense altar . . ." (NLT).

Appendix E

Chapter 5—Three Tribes Outside

The Census

Exodus 40:2, "On the first day of the first month you shall set up the tabernacle of the tent of meeting" (NKJV).

Numbers 1:1-4, "Now the Lord spoke to Moses in the Wilderness of Sinai, in the tabernacle of meeting, on the first day of the second month, in the second year after they had come out of the land of Egypt, saying: "Take a census of all the congregation of the children of Israel, by their families, by their fathers' houses, according to the number of names, every male individually, from twenty years old and above—all who are able to go to war in Israel. You and Aaron shall number them by their armies. And with you there shall be a man from every tribe, each one the head of his father's house" (NKJV).

Numbers 2:1-17, "And the Lord spoke to Moses and Aaron, saying: "Everyone of the children of Israel shall camp by his own standard, beside the emblems of his father's house; they shall camp some distance from the tabernacle of meeting.

On the east side, toward the rising of the sun, those of the standard of the forces with Judah shall camp according to their armies; and Nahshon the son of Amminadab shall be the leader of the children of Judah." And his army was numbered at seventy-four thousand six hundred. "Those who camp next to him shall be the tribe of Issachar, and Nethanel the son of Zuar shall be the leader of the children of Issachar." And his army was numbered at fifty-four thousand four hundred. "Then comes the tribe of Zebulun, and Eliab the son of Helon shall be the leader of the children of Zebulun." And his army was numbered at fifty-seven thousand four hundred. "All who were numbered according to their armies of the forces with Judah, one hundred and eighty-six thousand four hundred—these shall break camp first.

"On the south side shall be the standard of the forces with Reuben according to their armies, and the leader of the children of Reuben shall be Elizur the son of Shedeur." And his army was numbered at forty-six thousand five hundred. "Those who camp next to him shall be the tribe of Simeon, and the leader of the children of Simeon shall be Shelumiel the son of Zurishaddai." And his army was numbered at fifty-nine thousand three hundred. "Then comes the tribe of Gad, and the leader of the children of Gad shall be Eliasaph the son of Reuel." And his army was numbered at forty-five thousand six hundred and fifty. "All who were numbered according to their armies of the forces with Reuben, one hundred and fifty-one thousand four hundred and fifty—they shall be the second to break camp.

And the tabernacle of meeting shall move out with the camp of the Levites in the middle of the camps; as they camp, so they shall move out, everyone in his place, by their standards" (NKJV).

Appendix F

Chapter 6—Access

The Birth of Levi

Genesis 29:34, "She conceived again and bore a son, and said, "Now this time my husband will become attached to me, because I have borne him three sons." Therefore his name was called Levi" (NKJV).

Numbers 1:50, "Put the Levites in charge of the Tabernacle of the Covenant, along with all its furnishings and equipment. They must carry the Tabernacle and all its furnishings as you travel, and they must take care of it and camp around it" (NLT).

Numbers 1:53, "but the Levites shall camp around the tabernacle of the Testimony, that there may be no wrath on the congregation of the children of Israel; and the Levites shall keep charge of the tabernacle of the Testimony" (NKJV).

Deuteronomy 21:5, "Then the priests, the sons of Levi, shall come near, for the Lord your God has chosen them to minister to Him and to bless in the name of the Lord; by their word every controversy and every assault shall be settled" (NKJV).

Exodus 30:30, "And you shall anoint Aaron and his sons, and consecrate them, that they may minister to Me as priests" (NKJV).

Exodus 35:19, "the garments of ministry, for ministering in the holy place—the holy garments for Aaron the priest and the garments of his sons, to minister as priests" (NKJV).

Exodus 25:22, "And there I will meet with you, and I will speak with you from above the mercy seat, from between the two cherubim which are on the ark of the Testimony, about everything which I will give you in commandment to the children of Israel" (NKJV).

Numbers 1:49, "Do not include the tribe of Levi in the registration; do not count them with the rest of the Israelites" (NLT).

Zechariah 4:6, "Then he said to me, "This is what the Lord says to Zerubbabel: It is not by force nor by strength, but by my Spirit, says the Lord of Heaven's Armies" (NLT).

Exodus 40:15, "Anoint them as you did their father, so they may also serve me as priests. With their anointing, Aaron's descendants are set apart for the priesthood forever, from generation to generation" (NLT).

John 1:1, "In the beginning was the Word, and the Word was with God, and the Word was God" (NKJV).

Zechariah 4:6, "Then he said to me, "This is what the Lord says to Zerubbabel: It is not by force nor by strength, but by my Spirit, says the Lord of Heaven's Armies" (NLT).

Appendix G

Chapter 7—The Body

The Perfume Maker

Exodus 30:22-25, "Then the Lord said to Moses, "Collect choice spices—12-1/2 pounds of pure myrrh, 6-1/4 pounds of fragrant cinnamon, 6-1/4 pounds of fragrant calamus (cane), and 12-1/2 pounds of cassia—as measured by the weight of the sanctuary shekel. Also get one gallon of olive oil. Like a skilled incense maker, blend these ingredients to make a holy anointing oil" (NLT).

Exodus 30:25-29, "Like a skilled incense maker, blend these ingredients to make a holy anointing oil. Use this sacred oil to anoint the Tabernacle, the Ark of the Covenant, the table and all its utensils, the lampstand and all its accessories, the incense altar, the altar of burnt offering and all its utensils, and the washbasin with its stand. Consecrate them to make them absolutely holy. After this, whatever touches them will also become holy" (NLT).

Exodus 30:30, "Anoint Aaron and his sons also, consecrating them to serve me as priests" (NLT).

About the Author

Garry Stopa first received Jesus as Lord and Savior on August 21, 1988. He is very happily married and has four adult children and three grandchildren. Garry and his wife, Michelle, live in Abbotsford, British Columbia.

Garry has been semi-retired since 2008, collecting royalties for an invention and trading stocks and options. Very well equipped with computer Bible study tools and an abundance of time to study and listen to preaching, he presents his findings in books.

Garry Stopa has authored three other books to date:

- *The Day of Benjamin—What the Bible says about End Times Prophecy*
- *More Than Enough—Physical, Spiritual, and Emotional Benefits of Holy Communion*
- *Baptized in God—Baptism in the Holy Spirit*

To learn more visit:
www.booksbygarrystopa.com

If you would like to be part of the incredible plans God has for His people, just invite Jesus into your life. He wants to become personally involved in your life. Just pray this simple prayer:

> Lord Jesus, I believe You experienced a painful death for all the sins of this world. I want to become drenched in the Holy Spirit and receive everything You paid for me to have. Amen.

Start talking to Him as a friend who is always with you. He will speak to you through His Word, the Bible. Fellowship with Him by praying in tongues, and get to know Him personally; it is amazing!